SYMPATHY FOR THE COURIERS

Sympathy
for the Couriers

Peter Richardson

Signal
EDITIONS

SIGNAL EDITIONS IS AN IMPRINT OF VÉHICULE PRESS

Published with the generous assistance of The Canada Council for the
Arts and the Book Publishing Industry Development Program of the
Department of Canadian Heritage.

SIGNAL EDITIONS EDITOR: CARMINE STARNINO

Cover design: David Drummond
Photo of author: Simon Garamond
Set in Minion by Simon Garamond
Printed by Marquis Book Printing Inc.

LIBRARY AND ARCHIVES CANADA CATALOGUING IN PUBLICATION DATA

Richardson, Peter, 1948-
Sympathy for the couriers / Peter Richardson.
Poems.
ISBN 978-1-55065-234-5
I. Title.

PS8585.I1964S95 2007   C811'.54   C2007-904438-7

Published by Véhicule Press, Montréal, Québec, Canada
www.vehiculepress.com

Distribution in Canada by LitDistCo
orders@litdistco.ca
Distributed in the U.S. by Independent Publishers Group
www.ipgbook.com

Printed in Canada

For Michael Richardson
1940-2006

Acknowledgements

Some of these poems have appeared or will appear in:
The Antigonish Review, *The Dalhousie Review*, *Fiddlehead*, *Krax Magazine* (England), *The Malahat Review*, Pig Iron Series, *PRISM International*, *The Rialto* (England) and *Wisconsin Review*.

I am indebted to Martine Chapdelaine who has been so patient and thoughtful in her responses to these pieces as they evolved.

Thanks to Ken Victor for his sharp eye and cogent suggestions. His humor was appreciated.

Also thanks to the Other Tongue Group, a baker's dozen of eagle-eyed readers, and to my editor, Carmine Starnino, who has been thorough down the stretch.

Carolyn Richardson, Amy Handy and Penny Hoblin offered valuable comments.

As usual, the following background crew has my gratitude: Sophie Richardson, Robert Chapdelaine, Françoise Benguerel, Steven Reynolds, Michael Harris, Susan Gillis, Morgan Camley, Simon Dardick, Vicki Marcok, Lorraine Vallée, Laurent Vallée-Bélisle, and Alexis Vallée-Bélisle.

I wish to thank the *Conseil des Arts et des Lettres du Québec* for their support.

Contents

One

THE FIST-PUPPET'S SOLILOQUY

You have to look past my felt-tipped eyes,
my lolling tongue drawn by the granddad
or uncle who has talked too long at lunch
and knows he must entertain the toddlers
with his jabbering, magic-markered fist.

I am the last item on your list, the puppet
that costs nothing to make: the bogeyman
couched between worn index and thumb,
my snarl converted to a hayseed's guffaw.

Admit that I bear traces of inbreeding,
that my face and body must always be
an abomination to children of any age,
that it twists me up inside to hear them
clamor for more of my troll's antics.

If you like hearing cracker bromides,
say that I also favor arenas, imperial
banquets involving human sacrifice,
oblations to the god of spewing lava.

Demand for me rises as I'm washed off
another hand in another suburban sink.
Others are waiting in need of laughter.
It is time I dusted off my Punchinello
and swam out into a little sea of faces

with my disfigurement at stage center:
winded, bleary-eyed, yet discovering
after each pratfall, a dropper's-worth
of the bile which keeps me going.

PANTOUM OF THE WAN IRONIST

The slaves in me are celebrating.
They've taken over the guard towers.
I watch them from my camp chair
in the Civic Hall of Small Achievements.

They've taken over the guard towers.
I used to brag about my work ethic.
In the Civic Hall of Small Achievements,
it's hard to manage a bloodless exit.

I used to brag about my work ethic,
my knack for maintaining ironic distance.
"Just try to manage a bloodless exit,"
they jeer at me through a wreath of flies.

My knack for maintaining ironic distance?
A donkey's head hangs around my neck.
Jeers come at me through a wreath of flies.
Someone will have to answer to this mob.

A donkey's head droops around my neck.
Can I sweet-talk my way out the front door?
Someone will have to placate these guys.
They say: "Write with your hands on fire!"

Can I sweet-talk my way out the front gate
past this scraggly assemblage of scribes?
They say: "Write with your hands on fire!
Call the machine-shop floor and get help."

Past this scraggly assemblage of scribes,
there has to be a rarely seen sub-basement,
a shaking machine-shop floor of the self
where saucepans emerge as surgical tools.

Would I swear *that* if I weren't manacled
to this camp chair, being jeered?
Ha, I won't be cowed by a mob, and yet
the slaves in me are celebrating.

FIORD DREAM: NOTE TO MY PSYCHIC DOUBLE

Out there again last night
where the weatherbeaten cottages
overlook an arm of the sea,
I found myself hugging a jackpine.

It was the croquet I enjoyed most,
not the view from our lichened lawn.
Did I shock you by chucking our mallets
end-over-end off that windy promontory?

I guess one of us had to unwind.
You should try winging things.
Forget the Berlitz tapes next time.
You can't bone up on jibberish.

Any time you want to go back,
I'm ready to board that little coastal train
and put up with those codgers
who kept snooping around with clipboards:

white-haired Customs officials
with serge collars and a clanking combination
of ticket punch and psychrometer
they would swing up from a chain on their belts.

Next time we'll carry a letter
from the Governor's Palace. Seals
are what those fellows understand best;
and I don't mean those haranguing rookeries

we could hear past sundown,
hundreds of feet below us on the rocks
as we sat out there with our drinks
and overcoats, watching the eider ducks pass.

BREAKAGE

Whenever I find myself
coasting down train trestles
specially modified for metal treads or tires,

I always pull a steam whistle
to warn of my juggernaut passage
through a sleepy village or mining camp.

Sometimes my drilling foreman
waves a torch and screeches: "Whoa,
don't shift down now!" as I go chuffing by him

into the middle of a frozen swamp
which would be fine if an angry mob
from a nearby bunkhouse wasn't approaching.

Either that or the dream cancels out
with me waking up panting but otherwise
relieved as my half-track with bald front tires

careens off a precipice—its final
ka-boom muffled by ten feet of snow
and the snapping trusses of cottage roofs.

SCOOTER

Folded under your swinging arm, it might also be a theodolite
or a light anti-tank weapon concealed as puerile transportation.
Equip it with a motor and you're Edison on a busman's holiday.

Provided a wayward stork hasn't hexed its steering column,
press down on the spring-loaded thumb pedal and position it
over the pavement while standing free of the running-board.

Stoop over its way-low-though-fully-extended handle-grips,
over its nicked amber wheels that'll give it teensy clearance
but as post-atomic bric-a-brac make snappy tribal pendants.

What do you care, right? You're only the genie's assistant,
though some days you're so wound up with centripetal force,
you could mimic its side-swerving, hedge-clipping antics.

It's when you ride back with a fistful of junk mail and bills
and lift it over your lawn edge that it jettisons good faith,
swinging around in a tight arc to crack you in the ankle.

You must learn to be as methodical as a civil engineer,
who kneels to pencil in surrounding operational limits,
so that I-beams swung by crane don't deck a building.

NOTES TOWARDS A MARRIAGE OF TWO HANDS

The hand doesn't want to be ossified from the neck up.
Its chest is the toucan's ribcage. Its aural calling card,
the click-clack of marionette shoes across a tabletop.

Under the right tutelage, it might polish its coloratura.
Oh hand, I want to warble with you at Covent Garden.
Why do you wobble when you sort papers at a podium?

Ten rave headlines cannot be wrong about your pipes.
Therefore, keep yodelling over tabletops or desktops.
Take heart! Another hand keyed to yours warbles too.

It longs to pipe its grief into a packed opera house
but lacks your improbable gift for transformation,
your leap from forking up peas to penning arias.

It's standing here in the wings by heaps of azaleas,
wondering if you'll consent to sign its program
and motor with it to Margate for a view of the sea.

HABANERA

A few words for the robin, puffy-faced contralto of the ravine
whose notes swell as spring advances, reminding me of those
chesty gals who used to sing in the choir loft in Georgetown,

women whose vibratos juggernauted out of control, but who
made up for it with enthusiasm, who strained in their frocks
above thin clouds of incense to prepare us for the droning

responses, the Oh-God-I-am-not-worthies which we spoke
on our knees on folded-down benches. You linger too long
over antiphonal phrases but your voice is fail-safe. You are

the Ladies' Auxiliary, the Quilting Committee and Parish
Potluck of our backyard gully. We face you in lawn chairs.
We depend on your constancy, your selfless volunteer spirit,

your pat laying down of that eight-note intro to the Habanera,
the mezzo-soprano's entrance in *Carmen*, from which you go
into scraps of almost legible whippoorwill music. Why not?

Who says opera has to suppress your gift for improvisation?
Tin parrot of the under-story, you buck us up like war bonds,
ads for powdered milk, or ration cards for gasoline and sugar!

LATE PROPOSALS FROM MY MUSE

1.

You have to be willing to love the crumpled
face, the flattened nose, the doll's straw hat
placed at a rakish angle on my bony head.

2.

You have to make me prince of your city
and squire me around with a local beauty
who hangs on my cornice-climbing arm.

3.

You have to cross a stony archipelago
and see out from under bone shelving
that repels all but the last hangers-on.

4.

You have to sit in a circle of ashes
with a wolf's skullcap on your head,
draining off the last of the bone jelly.

5.

My kind too had songs, an origin myth,
toys made from the bones of large birds.
That is what you must learn to spin from.

Two

Lured by the brief deployment
of light infantry on the plain,
carrion birds rode thermals.
A line of approaching chariots
settled into acting as drovers
whipping their quarry seaward.
The front ranks of absconders,
who saw that they had at best
bought an extra quarter hour,
pitched about in the surf. All,
who could swim further out
or clung to those who could,
now shaded their eyes to look
over a bone-dry thoroughfare.
Double-timing over the sand,
those who had treaded water
saw that 50 could walk abreast
over piazzas of polished coral.
Pharaoh, pacing in agitation,
awaited an eye-witness report
from those in the high dunes,
who dismounted and gulped
and consulted with each other.
If they told him how the sea
appeared to boil, how sharks
wriggled tail fins and gnashed
teeth as they hung suspended
like objects from a glassworks,
would he be quietly outraged?
Are stone blocks hard to haul?
Better to come back limping,
or let the news precede them.
Let some credulous fisherman
among the peasant bystanders
rush back to the seat of power
with a breathless tally of facts:

Chariots were lost in the surf!
Arrows fell short of their marks!
Let that fool see the pet cheetah
switching its tail by the throne.
Let him take in all the wives,
aging advisors, court flatterers
and hear how his words echoed.
Not them. They weren't fools.
They were envoys, subalterns,
youthful rear-guard reservists
who dawdled above the water,
watching the slaves get away.

THE HIGH BARRENS FOLK AGREE IN PRINCIPLE
TO PUT A MOJO ON THE VALLEY DWELLERS

Up here? Dry taiga. Down there?
Grass-carpeted bottomlands under stars,
deer halting to decipher the wind
a few yards upstream from an orchard.

Lucky buggers—like the folks
eating pancakes in valley-clinging kitchens,
each gazing across mowed hay
at a tire swing rigged above the Winooski.

Fool them with a brown facsimile meander.
Make it look as wind-dimpled
and snarled with oxbows as it always does
when people wake in half-light,

stretching at dormer windows
to take in what runs through their village.
Let them hop into their vans,
all briefcases and aftershave, as the river

a brilliant fakery, changes skin.
At the town bridge let them turn on radios,
oblivious to the transformation,
kept unawares by an up-tempo love song.

Then let their whistling be less confident
as they reach the highway,
wondering if they've left wallets
or purses on a dresser top.

Let us, shivering on our bearberry heath,
decide when to send it back,
this meander of theirs that we've swiped
on a whim, before a holiday,

a whim that is more like a full blown need
to hear a particular brown current
sliding by our door sills while another
counterfeit current slides by theirs.

CORA WAITS FOR A BRIGHT IDEA
FROM HER BOYS

Even in the well-watered east
it will gall her to see the jobless
after karaoke night at the tavern
shrug at diminishing expectations.

She'll recall a childhood memory
of hands fluttering in holy water
as a man washed his ravaged face
before proceeding to an altar rail.

"The bottle owned him," she'll say,
and her sons will picture that town
where their welterweight grandpa
ventured into savings and loans.

Did resurrecting that scarecrow
keep them from leaving university
when their own father drove south
with a little slip of a diner waitress?

Better they chop up an old Packard
and weld it back into a tractor,
than motor into the heart of Dixie
with a dipsomaniac carhop.

She'll be rooting for her sons
the moment they shine their shoes
and act as though they had a right
to stand in line for a paycheck. She,

with her memories of scarlet fever
and her father's short-lived bank,
will lift her glass to the first sign
one of them has a bright idea.

STIPEND

Even with a cleaning woman
who scours everything in sight
and prepares Swedish meatballs
for your biannual house parties,
you haven't forgotten what it was
to mop and remop wooden steps
on a Sunday in Dubuque, Iowa,
the upper half of you bent level
with the middle step, the smell
of grease caught up in your hair,
while girls your age tittered by
on their way to an ice cream soda.
So when Elizabeth breaks down
in the midst of polishing silver,
you forget about stepping outside
to rake leaves into burning piles
as she tells you about her husband
who drinks when he comes off shift.
The litany of cusswords and slaps,
his penchant for throwing lamps,
keeps you from passing this off
as a bad patch in a marriage. She,
Elizabeth, swears in Swedish now,
but as you take her polishing rag
and guide her to the kitchen nook,
this woman who accepts a coffee
after shredding a wadded napkin,
you find you've seized on a plan.
You'll raise her salary by a third
but the raise will be paid in cash.
Let's call this a rainy day stipend,
you say, glancing up at the clock,
anticipating the smell of leaves
burning in large piles as you hum
and rake and light up a cigarette
in the Connecticut of the 1950s,

where, yes, there are still bastards
though, thankfully, the last ones
you had to wake up to each day
are well out of the picture now.
You had the short course on crap.
It began in 1923 with the hoarse
prattle of a snippy banker's wife,
who showed you to a mop bucket
and addressed you as *Little Miss
Welfare Beauty of Eastern Iowa,
who'd better cut a lower profile
if she knows what's good for her.
This isn't a vacation community.
We're not taking the waters here.
Dinners are served at 12 sharp.
Suppers at six, and I'll thank you
not to hum within this kitchen.*

PROFESSOR BASSO CHATS IT UP ON THE
OSLO-TO-ROME NIGHT FLIGHT

"To enter into this bare bones account, dear,
it helps to have the taste of iron in your mouth
as you go skittering down an icy embankment
towards an abbey half-veiled in gusting snow.
You might still reach it if you put on a sprint.
Then again the popping of light machine guns
means your chances depend on how sightlines
have been narrowed, how often the wind gusts,
how hard you run and how well you negotiate
the little stucco wall that surrounds the abbey.
Have you vaulted up out of the drifting snow?
Good. Wallow across to a trampled commons
where hooded monks are walking to vespers.
One of them makes a large, full-armed wave.
He braces open the door as you scuttle inside.
Does it matter why a patrol has been after you?
You could be the brother of a local insurgent,
the clodhopper older brother who likes snow
and goes walking in it after his factory shift.
Down onto your knees now and into a space
closed off by a plaster-covered panel. Hands
fluent in guiding the hounded urge you down.
You can hear a voice haranguing the monk,
telling him he'll need more than a good act
of contrition if he doesn't start speaking up.
You will learn that this is the assistant abbot
doing his best theatrical turn for the soldiers
bunched now in a snow-plastered delegation.
All of this happens as you are shaking, dear.
You are trying to control your bowels here,
and you, who work for a perfume company
distributing scents that float down bus aisles,
you would note all the odors in that closet.
A strong cologne of cat piss and old sweat

might mingle with crude lard soap and dust.
Whatever it was helped you avoid detection,
you'd embrace it and want it cancelled out.
Why? because that coat-of-arms-of-smell,
shielding you like a reactor's lead casing,
would not control the parade of memories
passing before you as you hunkered down
to wait out the staring duel between men
three feet from your stuccoed cubbyhole.

The pale eyes of the Wehrmacht sergeant
wondering if he can trust the older monk,
then deciding, *yeah, he's not putting us on,*
a drop of one degree of accumulated heat
in that cold, arched, half-lit hall, the slow
receding of boots and voices—all that
would not occur before you'd seen a film
of your many acts of petty-thievery, your
church-collection-box-emptying swagger
from pre-adolescence to this rat cabinet.
And that's where you'd want to be purged
of the over praised faculty called memory.
You would want to review only noble acts.
But since you ask, Signorina, since the war
remains clear to me through my eyes, ears
and nose—all of which are foundering, yet
good enough when it comes to awakening
the one horrendous moment—and since we
don't know each other except as travellers,
I'll tell you about my petty transgressions
what I did with my time away from work:
driving a catering truck past checkpoints
and into the yards of requisitioned villas
where German soldiers helped us unload
sides of ham and beef, cases of red wine,
how I was soon taken aside at the factory
told to wise up or kiss my ass goodbye
that if what I wanted was extra rations
or a special standing with the Fascisti

I could start measuring my own coffin
which made me an instant winter hiker,
lover of snowstorms, breaker of curfews,
a 20-year-old factory town know-it-all—
lucky enough to wash up in a monastery."

ABOUT RILEY

He was always there to get wind of it,
helpfully taking up the barbecue tongs
in a time of distress on landscaped lots
whenever marriages were on the skids.
You'd have noticed him in a courtroom.
Let me show you this block-party shot.
There, he's the one with the chef's hat,
the wiry lawyer who slept with women
whose friends, judging from their photos,
were the women he wanted to sleep with.
It's hard to fault him for that. He'd wake
in a strange bed and his eyes would see
a collage of photos on a bedroom wall.
One face of many would speak to him.
The rest was a question of when. How
long would it take him to connect? He
did have a winning way with men too,
hailing taxis, quick to give up his seat.
The wives? That's the supreme enigma.
It's as if they didn't want to betray him.
None of them wanted to let him down.
That is, of course, till he met my Meg.
She bedded him then spoke to a friend,
who spoke to a pal and the rest sounds
familiar except for the sheer numbers.
It's more like demographics. And yet,
the kicker is, he got A.L.S. so instead
of being booted out on his ass, Riley
wound up with round-the-clock care,
all us husbands sitting around almost
homicidal at this last coup de grâce,
him revved up at Brigham Memorial
receiving his fold like a dying Pope.
Imagine a room full of career moms
juggling two jobs and house chores,

spoon-feeding Riley spiked sherbet,
closing ranks whenever we bristled
as we did for months, us husbands,
reaping what we sleep-walked into.

MCFARLANE'S RECAP FROM SKYE

"They called me in and offered half-pay.
Topped up my last year to make it 25.
All in all, I ought to be grateful here
in this cottage on the peninsula road
with my view of gannets and puffins
across Blythe Strait. So I thank them.

'Horizons like yours can go off-kilter,'
said a friend of mine at the firm. Well,
he should know. He saw me chuck
a wastebasket across three cubbyholes
of accountants at the junior manager.

I'll navigate through a stormy winter,
watching the straight dives of ospreys.
To hell with Sundays at Sandown Park,
glassing the pack and thinking: 'Here's
my horse—fucked at the finish again.'
Give me a tight house in the Hebrides.

Come summer, I may renew the lease,
sell my mahogany hutch, buy a boat,
get myself better binoculars. 'Why not
a telescope?' my neighbor suggested.
She may be right. No nooky there, Pat.

She's ten years older and uses crutches.
We two are grand cohorts at Scrabble,
birders who can look out for each other.
I don't know how she's lasted out here
miles from the nearest druggist and pub.

You see how the mighty are fallen?
Newspapers take all day to arrive.
I get world events over a Guiness.
Darts aficionados want my name.
I've changed since I managed audits."

A NEIGHBOR RECALLS BARNEY CLARK

Recipient of the Jarvik-7 (1921-1982)

I wished him a donor heart
as soon as possible to replace
the ventricular device powered
by two air hoses snaking in

under his shirt. The clicking
I had to factor into small talk
almost didn't matter. Don't we
run on a stew of battery juices?

After guzzling tepid lime-aid,
he'd say he was selling bibles
or funeral insurance, his eyes
rolling half back in his head.

What could I do but go along
with his brittle jokes, asking
if he'd brought a policy along
for me to check its loopholes?

And yet there was that hissing
battery-powered compressor
that kept him up nights as if it
shared wires with a pipe bomb

strapped underneath his shirt,
and he, a Soviet-style defector
couriered secrets to a drop-off,
a safe house he never reached.

NOTES TOWARDS A BILLY BISHOP BIOPIC

Bishop might've begun on the prairies,
   a no-count station sweep
      with an unpaid saloon bill,
in 1915, a crack shot
   given a choice between
      learning wingovers,
or sitting in county lockup
   and hearing about the war
      from silver-haired deputies,

but he hailed from Owen Sound
   and in military college
      got caught using
crib sheets on a final exam,
   so the differences
      for cinematic purposes
are reconcilable. We have
   the raw material
      whether we ship him out

from the high plains or Georgian Bay;
   whether we fudge the details,
      or go so far as to doubt his
single-handed dawn raid
   on a German aerodrome
      in June of 1917—the time
he claimed to have shot up
   three Albatros single-seaters
      over farmland east of Vimy—

we still have the flying ace
   hobnobbing with Lady St. Helier
      on his leave in London,
the take-charge guy from Lake Huron
   by way of Toronto,

                    tea dancing with socialites
        halfway through the war,
                about to steam back to Canada
                    to see his dying father.

        We might want to show him weeping
                between missions just once,
                        yet raring to go aloft again
        as if a shorter period of recuperation
                improved his chances,
                        kept his gunnery skills sharp,
        the way gamblers feel
                they must stay at the table.
                    In the short but deadly

        salad days of aerial combat
                where no mention is made
                        of cockpit diarrhea
        and parachutes are too bulky
                to be anything but theoretical,
                        our four-mission-a-day man
        will post the highest numbers,
                downing 72 *Hun machines,*
                        noting coordinates in his log.

        Yet, we won't know what aerodrome
                received his low-level strafing,
                        and it's hard to explain
        why three of his former flying mates
                will refuse to sign an honorary
                        stamp issued 50 years later,
        commending his single-handed raid.
                Would we have had to be there,
                        cued to the unverifiable?

        Let him become Canada's air marshal
                in charge of flight recruiting
                        and halt the screenplay

short of his failed attempt
   to re-up as a fighter pilot
      for the Korean War.
Freeze-frame him over the trenches,
   reloading his Lewis gun,
      a lawyer's son with a mission,
      closing on a German triplane.

POSTSCRIPT

("...yes, we do print serializations. Sorry,
we couldn't give your sample chapters
the final green light. I hope you're well.")

If you're at this moment
standing on a window ledge
with a panoramic view,
let the policeman talk you
into his clutches by steps.
Don't be embarrassed after
stretcher bearers arrive
to wrap you up as if
for living mummification.
Come. Take a sideward step,
then another. This return
requires a new concentration
which we, at this magazine
of which I am the editor
and arbiter of all that's good,
hope you will rediscover
before the river wind
plucks you from your perch
ten stories above the traffic,
which we hope has not
been allowed to continue
blithely circulating below
as if you weren't in the direst,
dreariest fix. Take up
what little charm you had
before you received
our polite rejection note
and think of those, who
by accident of birth
aren't as fit or solvent
as you and yet abide
in some fleabag hotel.

What you set store by
more than most—a notion
of grace or perfection—
let that be your beacon
through the first week
of self-loathing and regret,
emotions you'd do better
not to contemplate
as you take your first
step in off that granite ledge,
followed by the first
of many histrionic-filled
relapses: sheets tied to sheets,
foiled escapes from wards,
staved off shock therapy.
Yes, at the fortress-like residence
where you find yourself
strapped to a surgical bed-table
and given a towel to bite on,
be thankful for the deal
a rich aunt steps in to broker,
ensuring your remanding
to a kinder institution
where macramé and knitting
stand in for flagellation
and the ward nurses
understand self-expression
in all its tawdry forms,
hiring local deacons
to give batik workshops,
followed, we hope
by ultimate recovery
and a tour of arts programs,
where your near plunge
may prepare others
for the rigors of rejection.

THE WIDOWED BIRDER SIGHTS
A MAY-DECEMBER PAIRING

As he watches groping
that isn't only tender
in the midday surf
and shakes his head
at the leap of faith
both must be making,
he reminds himself
that he too is past eighty
and wouldn't mind
for a minute being
squeezed back to life
by a trolling angel
along this strip of sand
known for its pelicans.
He will hunker down
and hear his heart
knock in his throat,
watching the bald
wingless biped whoop,
skip and scoop up
his confidante for a kiss.
A binocular circle
reiterates loss—*his*
not theirs—as the tide
wets her pink sarong
and sops his beige
trousers to the knee:
the octogenarian faun
and his shepherdess
a quarter mile away,
digging in their heels
as the surf drenches
and reconfigures them.

Three

THE LANDLOCKED SELKIE

She's eating out of a jar of whelks,
hip braced against our fridge door.
Upstairs is where she'll sleep it off
with earplugs to counter my snore.

We're together in this pick-me-up
end-of-day hunkering down to salt.
Only she needs a periodic pit-stop:
whelk flesh tops her off by default.

Let's hope we make the drive soon
to a double cot in a dock shed
where she can strip, take two steps
and dive to the cold clam bed.

Even cuttlefish do better than what
awaits her each morning at nine:
recycled air, word-counts to meet,
and not a whiff of salutary brine.

TEN TERCETS FOR LINKED HORNS

"I'd almost rather have horns,"
she says in the dark bedroom,
rubbing her head against mine.

"There would be that bawling
call from the rest of the herd
hailing us from a stonewall.

With just the right pressure
we could lessen the itching
brought on by all the flies."

"Mud would help that too,"
I say as I lower my head
to the specter of bluebottles

forming a cloud around us
and run my furrowed brow
along the length of her ribs.

I'm willing to consider this
anatomical alteration: horns
to graze against doorways in

the wee hours when I teeter
to the bathroom or hobble
downstairs at 3 AM. Let her

rub her forehead against me.
We'll be two head of cattle
sashaying down a fence line,

a day's batch of roughage
awaiting our grinding teeth,
companionability present

in a series of clicks—the rub
of her hard flat forehead
against my mud-flecked ribs.

A CONVALESCENT MOUNTAINEER AND HIS WIFE CONSIDER THEIR DAUGHTER'S ANTICS

(free-solo: v. to scale a rock face
without ropes or other implements.)

Him: She's lucky to be able to cling
to maple slats of shoulder height
and zip to that spot above the stereo.

Who wouldn't like permission
to climb the bannistered half-flight
along its carpeted outside edge?

Let's consider the angles. It's time
to bound up the outside of the stairs
with our daughter's blessing. Let her

sit here on the leather sofa's edge
paying out the rope of encouragement,
not knowing whether to applaud or

cringe. I hear you saying that's tilted
logic, dear. I admit. It fails every test
of responsible thinking. What then

should I, your broken-boned lummox,
do once I've bounded off this couch?
Should I take up free-soloing with

pumice bag and running shoes?
Maybe I need a crazier challenge.
Devil's Tower in under eight hours.

Her: Fine, Tenzing. Go wrestle a ledge.
Walk the Khumbo ice fields.
But if your adrenalin misfires again,

who says you'll land in hemlocks
and ten feet of snow
the way you did last April Fool's?

I don't want a gravel-voiced cop
speaking on behalf of rescuers
who found you crumpled up

at the bottom of a crevasse.
What about your sculpture sales?
Am I the one supposed to keep

your arctic hares, foxes and owls
rolling into collectors' dens
when they're boxed for exhibit

in vocational school gyms?
Who's going to clear our road
when a coastal storm hits?

Forget that hammock shelter
you sleep suspended in on days
when snow halts your descent.

I want you dug in here, for good,
watching our four-year-old
on that foolhardy route she takes
to a tobacco tin of pennies.

BATHROOM MIRROR

He keeps reaching forward to clear the glass of distortion
but already they are different from the way they were
in the shower. There's no groping-with-the-soap out here
under the fluorescent lights, only the two of them
correcting their postures as if this were a locket photo,
which, in a way, he supposes it is. She's asking him
to look at what little they know about the couple
whose habit of dazzling each other requires testing
in rooms of all dimensions and all manner of lighting.
He reaches forward to wipe again. Then his hand
drops to encircle her waist. He likes what she hopes
he will see when they look at themselves in composure.
And maybe they do make a couple who can acquire
a habit of appreciating this after water has sluiced
down their bodies and foamed into a steel drain.
Maybe she will always tug him forward by the towel
and his hand will go on alighting at her waist
till they are ragged with this continued hydrotherapy
through decades of soapy postcoital showers.
Right now, she holds him to a three-quarters hug.
Le beau couple, she says. *Regarde le beau couple.*

COASTAL HOLIDAY

You dreamed we had an idiot child,
a girl over six feet tall who had to be
led by the elbow down an esplanade
and along a crescent of stony beach.
She was the blank look on our faces,
the gawp that besets us at breakfast
when a single misunderstood word
scrambles what the other has said.
With her arms raised and waggling,
she snorted at our repeated efforts
to clip leashes to her trouser loops.
Hotel guests had been afraid of her
but on the beach, two donut vendors
thought she was terrific and said so.
They liked her bug-eyed promise,
her fluency in imitating our balky
attempts to rise beyond entry-level
competence in the other's language.
We allowed ourselves to be flattered
and led her up a long forested slope
full of hidden speakers belting out
jug band tunes from the last century.
The twangy washtub bass irked us
but when we saw how it mesmerized
our daughter, we lowered ourselves
to the moss under the trees, our hands
making small talk as she banged out
a rhythm to the buzzing of cicadas.

ON JFK PARK

It was easy reversing "The Star Spangled Banner" to draw
laughter. Be glad someone had a shag carpet and you sat
on her scarred piano bench—bare toes in wispy white pile,
consenting to sing your national anthem backwards during
the imaginary rewind of a war film whose closing melody
never failed to morph you into a crazed Russian librettist.

Be glad of it and stop qualifying the good times when they
came and went in almost glitch-free cycles with her sons
jostling on the couch to hear you sing skewed quatrains
or play the harmonica or mimic a man with cerebral palsy
jittering across the floor as if his mobility depended on
old-time switchboard operators who misrouted each call.

Weren't you enlisted as crackpot caretaker of glee so that
all three siblings, aged 8, 10 and 12, would be cramped
with giggles during a rainy Sunday of indoor moping,
a fact you later felt sheepish about since what stepfather
in his right mind would send up a handicapped person
if not someone pandering to a cackling inner demon?

It was you and you enjoyed it: the narrow back flower bed
where you weeded her few frowsy ferns that got two hours
of sunlight three months of the year and where you set up
her gas-fired barbecue during the hottest days of summer,
the six of you, if you count her daughter, sojourning there
in that shotgun flat that gave onto a city park with a pool.

Why rue the limitations of anything even the horseplay
that degenerated into slugfests? Between her three sons
there was an understanding, and you sanctioned it, till
she would return fuming into her sepia-toned parlor
haranguing you to please set the tone and act your age
for the boys you wished could be transported to Manila.

Yes, sent to Manila never to return till they had learned
Spanish and taken wives as hard-headed as their mom,
who'd teach them to be coronet players or salesmen
schooled in mores they weren't going to learn in the
flat on Kennedy park with you reversing the anthem
and gibbering across the living room in a pretend palsy.

RUE WISEMAN

Like a Chinese box whose lever has been found
under a sliding section of lacquered wood,
you go from lying beside me on your back
to curling with your back towards me.

A figure has been arrived at that exceeds
expenses and output. Production is unhappy
and will soon be calling back its salesmen
from the silk-curtained suites of jade merchants.

TUCK RETURNS AIRSIDE AGAIN

Five years into retirement,
he strolls down the ramp
hallway with its busted
office chairs and hidden
domestic dramas. Who

better qualified than he
to grasp how the exodus
of gung-ho card players
has to do with the influx
of these shaved-headed,

pup-faced replacements:
men who adjust voices
to the sudden spiking
of decibels as airbuses
pull up at right angles
to the grimy windows?

He wants to abide here,
a chipper gent speaking
about outdated aircraft
and their peculiarities
at a table in the newly

renovated lunchroom
with its row of ovens
chiming *dinner's ready,*
him twinkling with his
airside visitor's permit.

AIRPORT MISDIAL

Given his aptitude for one-digit mistakes,
he can't help imagining
others the Fates have touched this way:
convention-goers certain

they were being connected with an agent
about to offer assistance
with flight departures or arrivals,
instead of this rerouting

to transport of quite another kind offered
with such enthusiasm
he has to wonder if the girl on the tape
isn't living the good life,

racking up multiple bonus flying miles
when she isn't consulting
her broker about smart money funds.
How else to explain this:

Hey, Fly boy, want the ride of your life?
My name's Angie and I'm
waiting for you to be my cockpit guide
as we hump over Waikiki.

I'm already half out of my tank top...
which is where his thumb
depresses the phone's "off" button,
abridging the message,

leaving it in breathy suspension. Though
now he thinks of those
who've set this number on direct-dialing:
buyers of ecstatic tidings

whose noisy midway he's stumbled onto
in his west-facing room
with its late summer screeches of gulls,
chuckles of starlings.

I SING OF THE VULCAN

six-barrelled sanitizer of drop zones,
capable of firing 1200 rounds a minute,
wing-mounted aerial weed-whacker,

tested at the National Guard firing range
in far off Underhill, its wide kill-radius
hinted at over the valley rumor mill.

Plum descendant of the Gatling gun,
a three-second snatch of throat-singing
flung at me from beyond the Notch,

beyond Jeffersonville and Cambridge.
If I heard it now, it would be a sound
linked to memory: my 16-year-old self

trimming fir trees for Christmas sale
in that squelchy Vermont bush lot
I worked in one delinquent summer,

while a cough from over the hills
signed itself in the air, an underground
bellows teasing sparks from a forge,

a god working that bellows, stamping
his bunioned feet and chuckling
at nonstop rush orders for sky armor.

MY FATHER IN RETIREMENT

When happy for no reason, he'd clap
his hands together once. The left
thumb and forefinger would then
embrace the right thumb and move
along its length till they had gone
beyond the object of their hugging.
Both hands would then draw back
and clap again, repeating the clinch
of the right thumb: his gesture of
affirmation, his day's opening up,
giving him the leeway he needed
to trace the performance of shares
whose dividends gave our lives
their charmed rusticity or plunged
our little ark into doubt. As snow
fell earlier and melted later than
it did on the three acres my mother
recalled with nostalgia, he'd clap
his hands and mutter something
prescient about Rome's not being
built in a day as I looked up from
homework and kept my expression
neutral watching him applauding
as no other father would applaud
for the sake of hearing his palms
smack and twist apart—smarting
from the damp of a three-season
room with its view of mountains
and its list of stocks appreciating
or depreciating in the fine print
of a newspaper spread on a table.

Four

KITCHEN SONG

(After an oral description of itinerant
butchers from the Po river valley.)

Grab your biggest pot,
set up the tripod,
throw in an onion,
the *noccini* are coming.

Invite your uncles,
lug out the accordeon,
pass the sweetbreads,
the *noccini* are coming.

On their rickety bicycles,
in the dead of winter
with their black capes
over the white fields,

the *noccini* are pedalling
from Parma this morning.
Go out and meet them.
Set out the meat hooks.

The old sow can smell them,
can sniff out the lung blade
before they approach her
in the muddy paddock.

Let's not have a replay
of last year's fiasco
when one boar bolted
and trampled Pietro.

Go wake up Grandpa,
who still misses opera.
Set him up in the parlor
with grappa and a victrola.

The *noccini* are coming
with their cleavers and dirks
and abattoir savoir-faire
in the blade-wielding wind.

THE BALLAST TRUNK

You haul it on a sledge. The tools inside it tinkle,
making the sound metal makes when it is jounced
hard over stream bottoms as you ford and reford
the same creek, a man adept at coffering loss,
at keeping it snug in numbered drawers. You halt,
turn and wade back across the cold wide brook.

You know you can't decide on a name for this
till you acknowledge the way of the trunk,
what the ropes for pulling it request of you, how
it feels to have pulled it without a breather,
straining into the draglines as a passing cloud
gives you a glimpse of your clenched jaw.

Scraping along in the slow current though,
you see how ballast can be helpful in grieving.
It joins you to the gravelled, sun-splotched
pools your trunk rudders over, not to mention
the ruckus of stirred brook stones, the hard
jangling ride your tools take under hemlocks.

Your last-second lurches to maintain balance
flog you forward, while the rocking motion
a horse might make here grinds at your back.
There's something to be said for not knowing
whether to set up camp, or continue hauling
till you've gouged a channel down to bedrock.

OAK LEDGE PARK IN DECEMBER

Burlington, Vermont

The cove that was like a quilt
studded with pieces of mirrors

that kept breaking up as I stood
on an outcrop of reddish stone,

continues to shatter and slide,
craze and stack against itself

long after I have crossed over
the ice-narrowed St. Lawrence,

unpacked my duty-free smokes,
drifted off to bebop and awoken

dry-mouthed in the city dark
to the thunk of a sidewalk plow.

This I can report has escaped
detection on the road north: fog

blowing through lakeside oaks,
air moving through sere lungs,

and, under my heels as I knelt
listening to those blocks of ice,

the gnarled anchors of the trees
hauling up a dark, chalky gruel.

LAURENT FACE TO THE RAPIDS

The day he pulled himself upstream,
his mother made a sign to me
not to think of intervening.

I had been about to shout warning
or praise—neither of which
would have roped him in.

Spread-eagled over the current,
he took a few handholds,
not so much to climb

as to feel what might drag him back
and stove in a rib if he let go.
It was his attention

I meant to speak of and his mother
shushing me as he crept
higher up the rapids,

free-soloing up the Doncaster,
clenched over the current,
foothold by foothold,

till we sensed he had absolved
us, the watchers, from being
useless on the sidelines

and joined the class of those
who like to work up close
to their material,

notching small advances
with a tilt of the head
or a loud grunt.

He searched for and found
rock shelving he could
cling to—cracks

in riverine granite that would
enable his slow climb
to a spillway,

back of which, we later saw,
was a shoulder-deep
catch basin

where he could loll and replay
the effort before rising
to toss back

his 16-year-old's dreadlocks,
climb out under pines
and descend to us.

BUSTLE

Relate how he had to outclass the field at those nepotistic
job competitions whose winners were always the family
of other firemen, how anyone who hoped to ride a truck
or open a hydrant in that world had to be a fire-breather,

a fanatic, a go-for-broke, all-battalion risktaker who could
change channels at an interview and appear dispassionate,
how that was learned over a series of interviews, a series
of job competitions whose winners played the right note.

Recount his alternative to that long-shot job choice, how
he would study with a group of aspiring paramedics to be
versed in mouth-to-mouth resuscitation and the use of the
defibrillator to jumpstart flagging octogenarians and young

traffic accident victims, the ones he preferred to forget. Say
how he could whomp the breath back into you with his wide
hands placed just so over your sternum as you lay sprawled
under a flaking stucco ceiling or a leafless sidewalk maple,

this stepson of yours whose boots you keep wearing against
the day when you will have to replace the laces. Admit that
once the laces go it will be time to put the boots by the curb,
to let yourself be absolved of further compliance with some

rankling need to wear the boots down to their steel shanks,
which is not to gainsay the comfort of well-fitting footgear,
of kicking pallet dolly locks up or down, of booting chocks
out from under a nosewheel. How well these both did that

for you during your last days of workplace exertion. And yet,
accept that once your stepson finally did get his coveted job,
once he could sit all day in a fire hall with a book in his lap,
making a third again as much as a rookie ambulance driver,

how that was death for him who had to keep moving, feet
locked in a soaring broad-jump over an icy porch railing,
or pointing downwards towards the fields of St. Canute,
in freefall, his chute about to open and give him gravity.

VALEDICTORY

for Vincent-Xavier, 1980-2002

Klipspringer, Katzenjammer,
why don't you roll over
and adjourn this with laughter,
with a whinnying wail?

Speed us in kayaks down a river
north of Nominingue,
woodland biker, broad jumper,
fireman-in-training.

Reach up and tweak our ears
ahead of the coroner's
white coat, stethoscope
and actuarial calm.

Wrest that paramedic's tube
out of your clenched jaw.
Will that braid of contusions
off your macraméd neck.

Delete this day and all its hours,
reverse step, back up.
Take down that chinning bar
from your stairwell.

THE STATION CLOCK

ticks way ahead of itself and gongs
at intervals neither of us can reckon
since she padded down those stairs
to my cellar and rescued the thing,

which she then cradled to herself,
ascending with her trademark step
to this room where we can lie back
and fill the house with dependents

who, like her, will want to preserve
salvaged antiquities so as to hear
the hours vetting important news
quicker than we can toe tap it.

SOUTH PROSPECT FOLIO

1. April 27th

At 66, you went out under a new moon.
A glass of white wine, tilting sideways,
followed you in your sack-of-potatoes
fall to the deck overlooking your lawn.
The air was crisp. You felt a fluttering
and then you were given a long night
without a sheet draped over your face,
or straps buckled over that wide chest.
These and a toe tag would come later
after a cursory attempt to find a pulse.
Crows would offer grouchy greetings,
while a nephew slumbered on upstairs.
You would've been dead under clouds
as first light sketched in the lakeshore.
Far below you there would have been
herons settling into the cold shallows,
sentinels at their sunup starting points.

2. Vigil Decision

Ferreting out the right plan will mean
sitting in your side yard till morning,
the group of us hunkered in blankets,
your coffin braced by two sawhorses.
And since you liked rituals reduced
to a barefooted circling of a bonfire,
we'll forgo what a sexton could do,
who, in any case, has enough work
tending his brass-railed necropolis.
We'll put your carcass into a pickup
for a windy ride down the interstate
past mountains you liked to look at

to one of those yet-to-be-franchised
furnaces whose talkative custodian,
working out of the back of his barn,
will flick away a cigar, shake hands
and reduce your good bones to ashes.

3. Epic

What am I trying to compile here,
a gumshoe's account of the scene?
That no furniture was overturned
means our victim didn't struggle.
Who says an abridged biography
didn't pass before him as he fell?
I'm for high-tech special effects
where the falling pilot glimpses
his childhood through a cracked
windscreen as he clears a suburb
to crash in an abandoned quarry.
A time-lapse film of an oak tree
would show us decades trimmed
and cropped to a leisurely yawn.
Maybe that's what Michael saw:
his acorn self to his last breath
pitched at him in a split-second.

4. Jovial Host

Did you once take an air force exam?
That was one of those odd Plan B's
upstaged the moment you qualified
to network in Brazilian Portuguese.
In the Mato Grosso, you soaked up
dialects, soft-selling the benefits
of malaria vaccines or a generator.
Scroll ahead 30 years and I see you

doffing an affordable housing fez,
hacking through a jungle of grants
with Club Monk as your avocation,
something to fill the evenings with:
a no-frills camp for aging hippies
primed to summer beyond the grid.
No matter it never panned out. I can
see huts around a back country lake,
you ringing a dockside dinner bell.

5. Sibling Communiqué

Looking west from a corner window,
I was thinking in a countdown mode.
You were taking a last sip of Chablis.
Another day gone in the lives of those
who live on Planet Earth, I muttered.
You were falling against vinyl siding.
I was extemporizing about limits. *Yes,*
we're acolytes of the finite, I thought.
Hours north of the rudderless boat of
your body stretched out under clouds,
I was turning to my wife and daughter
who were downstairs whooping it up.
A lit window caught cards being dealt.
Later, we three would sleep and wake
refreshed—the phone ringing for me
after a mid-morning run, after seeing
a buck in the chest-high poplar whips.

Notes

For his single-handed dawn raid on a German aerodrome on June 2, 1917, Billy Bishop received the Victoria Cross.

The Doncaster river is in Quebec's southern Laurentians. The section of it referred to in "Laurent Face to the Rapids" is between Ste. Marguerite and Mont Rolland.

Any similarity between the Isle of Skye and the island location in "McFarlane's Recap From Skye" is fortuitous.

Signal
EDITIONS

Carmine Starnino, Editor
Michael Harris, Founding Editor

HIDE & SEEK Susan Glickman
MAPPING THE CHAOS Rhea Tregebov
FIRE NEVER SLEEPS Carla Hartsfield
THE RHINO GATE POEMS George Ellenbogen
SHADOW CABINET Richard Sanger
MAP OF DREAMS Ricardo Sternberg
THE NEW WORLD Carmine Starnino
THE LONG COLD GREEN EVENINGS OF SPRING Elisabeth Harvor
FAULT LINE Laura Lush
WHITE STONE: THE ALICE POEMS Stephanie Bolster
KEEP IT ALL Yves Boisvert (Translated by Judith Cowan)
THE GREEN ALEMBIC Louise Fabiani
THE ISLAND IN WINTER Terence Young
A TINKERS' PICNIC Peter Richardson
SARACEN ISLAND: THE POEMS OF ANDREAS KARAVIS David Solway
BEAUTIES ON MAD RIVER: SELECTED AND NEW POEMS Jan Conn
WIND AND ROOT Brent MacLaine
HISTORIES Andrew Steinmetz
ARABY Eric Ormsby
WORDS THAT WALK IN THE NIGHT Pierre Morency
    (Translated by Lissa Cowan and René Brisebois)
A PICNIC ON ICE: SELECTED POEMS Matthew Sweeney
HELIX: NEW AND SELECTED POEMS John Steffler
HERESIES: THE COMPLETE POEMS OF ANNE WILKINSON, 1924-1961
    Edited by Dean Irvine
CALLING HOME Richard Sanger
FIELDER'S CHOICE Elise Partridge
MERRYBEGOT Mary Dalton
MOUNTAIN TEA Peter Van Toorn
AN ABC OF BELLY WORK Peter Richardson
RUNNING IN PROSPECT CEMETERY Susan Glickman
MIRABEL Pierre Nepveu (Translated by Judith Cowan)
POSTSCRIPT Geoffrey Cook
STANDING WAVE Robert Allen
THERE, THERE Patrick Warner
HOW WE ALL SWIFTLY: THE FIRST SIX BOOKS Don Coles
THE NEW CANON: AN ANTHOLOGY OF CANADIAN POETRY
    Edited by Carmine Starnino
OUT TO DRY IN CAPE BRETON Anita Lahey
RED LEDGER Mary Dalton
REACHING FOR CLEAR David Solway
OX Christopher Patton
THE MECHANICAL BIRD Asa Boxer
SYMPATHY FOR THE COURIERS Peter Richardson
MORNING GOTHIC: NEW AND SELECTED POEMS George Ellenbogen

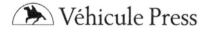 Véhicule Press